ALMOST and ALWAYS

Almost almost won the race

But Almost never did

Because he never ran the race

But only ran and hid

For Almost was afraid to lose

And afraid to win

So Almost never tried at all

When everyone else did

And some of them they lost that race

But one of them he won

And every single one of them

Had loads and load of fun

But Almost never had that fun

Although he almost did

Because he never ran that race

He only ran and hid

Then Almost went down to the sea

To swim the ocean blue

But the water frightened him

And swim he did not do

So while the other racing kids all swam together with glee

Almost sat alone on shore staring out to sea

But Almost wasn't done quite yet

He went to climb a tree

But thought the branches looked too high

So just sat in the leaves

And all the racing swimming kids they climbed that tree so high

And left poor Almost on the ground to gaze up at the sky

Almost thought I'll fly a plane to touch the clouds up there

But never left the runway because rain was in the air

Instead he said, "I'll fly a kite up in the sky so high"

But changed his mind and left to find something else to try

And so the day it came and went with everything to do

But Almost never did a thing not even tie his shoe

For Almost doesn't really know what Almost really likes

Because he never tries new things mostly out of fright

The lesson of Almost is this if you've listened well and true

When you *almost* everything, you never *really* do!

Now Always always tried her best

The best that she could do

And always ran in every race

And swam the ocean blue

Always always climbed a tree

With all the other kids

And never sat all by herself

Wishing that she did

Always flew planes in the sky

And touched the clouds up there

And tasted rain upon her tongue

When rain was in the air

And always flew a kite she'd found up in the sky so high

It circled around the world 3 times she counted with her eyes

And every day that came and went with everything to do

Was always met by Always and her 'Can do' attitude

And Always she was happy

Because she always tried

And even when she didn't win

Or fell down and then cried

She knew that she had had some fun

Or learned something brand new

Or made a friend

Or saw something

That others seldom do

The lesson of Always is this if you've listened well and true

When you Always do your best your best will always do!

WANT and DIDN'T

Want wanted everything much more than you or me

Want wanted more than one he wanted 2 or 3

Of everything he saw and thought that he could soon possess

For Want he thought that having things would make him feel the best

And so Want bought so many things Want really didn't need

He bought 3 cars, 2 trucks, 4 boats, a house and 10 TVs!

He bought all sorts of games and toys so much it made him stagger

He bought all kinds of rings and things he bought food by the platter

And if he bought the same thing twice it really didn't matter

Want bought and bought and bought and bought himself into a lather

Cause Want he had a hole inside that wanted to be filled

A hole that made him feel unwell even when not ill

He did not know just what it was or why he felt this way

But found that when he bought something it kind of went away

But this hole it never stayed away for very long

And every time that it came back it came back very strong

So Want would buy another thing a lamp, a desk, a chair

Dinosaur bones, a toaster oven, or clippers for his hair

A piece of art, a place to park, a plane not in the air

A tube of glue, a kangaroo, and one time the whole fair!

And so poor Want he spent his days just buying things in droves

And put them all inside his hole hoping it would close

But wanting more and more and more didn't make it go away

Instead it grew and grew and grew until there came a day

It got so big it swallowed Want who could not get away

And all the things he sought to own own him until this day

Cause wanting more and more and more

And wanting more and more things

Is just a way to lose yourself

To the hole that wanting brings.

****

Now Didn't didn't think this way he didn't want for more

Didn't was a happy boy who never wanted 4

Or 3 or 2 or 1 of something to make him feel alright

He was happy within himself morning, day and night

For Didn't knew one special thing that Want he did not know

That happiness comes from inside and not from things to show

So Didn't didn't have a hole that wanted to be filled

And Didn't wasn't swallowed up just like some tiny pill

By all the things he didn't need or want or didn't gather

Because he knew like me and you what's inside is what matters.

RUMOR and REASON

Rumor knew a thing or two

She said was about me

And told two other girls at school

Or maybe it was three

It may have been as many as seven

I really don't recall

But Rumor told all of them it

When I came down the hall

Then Rumor told another tale

About a girl named Mary

And whispered it to all the kids

Who then thought Mary scary

But Rumor wasn't done just yet

She hadn't rumored Sally

So Rumor told another rumor

That Sally liked John Malley

Sara and Beth

And Sam and Tess

They all were on her list

Mike and Stan

And Max and Pam

Not one of them was missed

Aidan and Bella

And Frances and Stella

All heard rumors that day

As Rumor's rumors were passed around in a rumor sort of way

And no one knew if any were true

Though it really didn't matter

Because she had upset us all

With her constant rumor chatter

Then finally Reason came into season and said with a rational voice

"I've heard Rumor's rumors and don't see the humor in her rumor spreading choice

For Rumor you've rumored all of these things though none of them are true

Because you've made up all of them as Rumors often do

But if you deceive, with rumors like these, you'll find it's always true

That one fine day I do dare say . . . the rumor will be about you!"

Now Rumor listened to Reason's words and knew what she now had to do

"I'll stop all my lies and I promise you guys with my rumors I'm finally through"

And all of us we sang and danced and were happy to be free

From Rumor's rumors about us all . . . but especially about ME!

LISTEN

Listen is a boy I know I see him every day

He is my light my love my joy in every single way

He is my sun my moon my stars he makes me feel alright

He is my morning afternoon my daybreak and my night

Listen is a perfect boy except in one small way

Listen doesn't listen to a single word I say

If I say, "It's morning time" he sleeps the day away

If I say, "It's breakfast time" he wants his lunch time tray

If I say, "We'll go tomorrow" he yells "Let's go today!"

If I say, "We'll leave right now" he cries "We have to stay!"

If I say, "Play time is over put your toys away"

He bellows and moans and eventually groans, "But I like my room this way"

And if I ask him to close the thing that he's opened it likely won't be done

To Listen it seems that opening things is much much much more fun

But when I say softly into my coffee "It's been a long and difficult day"

He stops what he's doing and all his boo-hooing in his most concerned little way

"Don't worry mommy and don't be so sorry it's going to all be okay . . . I'm gonna be good just the way that I should" and he does not look away

Then my little man takes hold of my hand, til he's sure that I am okay . . . and he gives me a hug, my one little bug, in his sweetest Listening way

Yes Listen is a boy I know I see him every day

He is my light, my love my joy in every single way

He is my sun, my moon my stars he makes me feel alright

He is my morning afternoon my daybreak and my night

And Listen is a perfect boy in the most perfect way

He listens when it matters most and I love him just this way.

BULLY and BRAVE

A Bully follows me around I hate to have to say

From my house to school and back most every single day

No matter what I try to do, or do or do not say

My Bully won't leave me alone - not for just one day

Cause Bully is the onlooker who looks the other way

When I'm scared and I need help but "Help!" I'm scared to say

And Bully is my neighbor who pretends he does not to see

When everyday I'm pushed around by 1 or 2 or 3

Other kids who call me names or stick things in my hair

Or trip me when I'm walking by or steal my lunch to share

Amongst themselves with none for me it simply isn't fair

But I'm scared to say something when no one seems to care

Bully is the janitor who eats lunch on the stairs

When kids at school they take my shoe to play catch in the air

I know that he could stop them if he wanted or he tried

But each day he turns away and just goes back inside

And Bully he's my soccer coach who always lets it pass

When other kids they choose up teams and always choose me last

Bully is the kids that laugh when other kids they say

That I smell funny or I'm a dummy until I run away

And while I know real friends would never say such things to me

Their teasing hurts me even more than even I believe

I know a friend is someone who's supposed to just be there

By your side who never hides no matter what I hear

But I know that I don't have these kinds of friends at all

For no one walks beside my side when I walk down the hall

And most of them they laugh and point at me most every day

And some of them they tell me that they wish I'd go away

But where am I to go I've asked myself if I don't stay?

When everywhere I go I find a Bully in my way

A Bully does not have to be the one who sadness brings

The one who pulls or kicks or trips or any of these things

The biggest Bullies that I know don't say or do a thing

When other Bullies bully me . . . and that's what really stings

My Bully's simply everyone . . . it's sad but plain to see

So everyone I'm begging you . . . please stop bullying me.

****

Lift up your head and dry your sad eyes

And listen to me and not bullies' lies

I have heard your prayers and your cries in the night

And I've come from the future to show you the light

Of a future that's out there for you and for me

A future of two not one against three

Believe what I tell you believe and you'll see

You were never meant to just be bullied

For I am Brave and I came to portend

That the days of your bullying are soon at an end

These bullies will change you'll see that it's true

And the meanness in them that's directed at you

Will ebb and subside a bit every day

As they grow and mature and eventually stray

From the childish acts of their childish minds

And a conscience develops in them over time

A conscience not blind to the damage they do

To the ones that they've bullied who've done nothing to

Them to deserve to be bullied like this

It will drive them to stop and to lower their fists

The silent ones too who laugh and who stare

Who gnaw on their tongues when they should show care

Will find a new voice they don't yet know they have

And use it together to shout down the bad

For I am Brave and I came here to say

That your future it holds such brilliant days

Such shining moments you just can't yet see

Believing in them is believing in me

Cause I'll be your shoulder when you're feeling blue

And I'll hold your hand when you're needing me to

We'll stand there together so proud and so tall

And we'll walk side by side down life's many halls

I'm the one in the future that's meant just for you

And I'm waiting out here in need of you too

Our futures are bound together you see

But there is no us without you and me

So you have to be brave and make it to me

As much as you can as much as can be

For I am Brave and I came here to say

That I hear you . . . I'm near you . . . and you'll be okay.

WHY and BECAUSE

I have a boy named Why who asked me why the world was round

And long before I'd even answered why a clock was wound

He asked me why his grandma's chin was always really saggy

He asked me to explain to him why mommy married daddy

He asked me why and how it was that birds flew in the air

And every now and then again why it was rude to stare

He often wanted me to say how plants and trees they grew

And why it was it took 2 laces to tie a single shoe

Every time it rained he'd ask me why rain fell in drops

And every time he ate one, why popsicles don't pop

He asked me all the standard ones like why the sky was blue

And every single day it seemed why he had to clean his room

He asked me all the crazy ones like why cats have 9 lives

He asked me all the hard ones too like why people tell lies

And looking at our dog one night he asked why she can't talk

And one day after visiting him why Grampa couldn't walk

And then one day he asked me why our God would let us cry

And followed that by asking me why one day we must die

I did my best to answer him but found the more I did

I got 10 times as many whys from my inquisitive kid

"I'm sorry Why", I finally said, "But I don't know these things

I maybe know a few of them like why a bee sting stings

But I can't say just what it is that God has up his sleeve

Or where we go after we die or if our spirits leave"

And then at last I said, "Why if we all knew everything,

Then come tomorrow morning . . . what would the morning bring?

There would be nothing new for us and life would be no fun

Because we'd know how it turned out before it had begun

So sometimes we just have to say that we just do believe

When we don't know just where we go when it's our time to leave"

Then Why he looked straight up at me as if a bell had rung

And repeated what I'd said to him, "So life would be no fun?"

I shook my head from side to side hoping we were done

"It's fine if you don't know why dad but tell me then . . . how come?"

"Well . . . . because."

MESSY and CLEAN

Messy was the messiest girl you'd ever want to see

Her room looked like a garbage dump from sea to shining sea

You couldn't see the floor at all her bed was all in tatters

But to Messy that was fine since neatness didn't matter

"I like my mess I must confess" she said it almost daily

"It lets me know just where I've been or where I have been lately"

"But Messy" Messy's mom would say, "one day you'll see its true

That being messy like you are will end up hurting you!"

Still Messy didn't care at all how messy she could be

Because her mom would clean it up e-ven-tu-al-ly

But just as soon as Messy's mess was cleaned up by her mom

Messy's mess would grow again before too very long

If Messy she had sticky hands she'd wipe them on her clothes

And if she had a tickle there her finger picked her nose

If Messy had mud on her shoes she'd track it on the floor

And any dirt upon her hands would end up on the door

If Messy's clothes were stained with food she really didn't care

And when she had a sticker she would stick it in her hair

If Messy had a piece of gum that had run out of flavor

She'd stick it to her dresser drawer saving it for later

If Messy spilled a glass of juice while running down the hall

She'd skip away and off she'd play not worrying at all

And when she had a pen or pencil but no piece of paper

She'd draw instead upon the wall because no one could make her

Be more neat or ever treat a thing with just good care

For Messy was a hopeless mess . . . until one day a bear

Found his way to Messy's home he'd smelled the mess inside

And followed it to Messy's room where she had run to hide

Slowly, oh so slowly, that bear entered Messy's room

As Messy hid beneath her mess shaking in the gloom

With one big paw he scooped it all and swallowed that mess down

Then burped aloud and looking proud that bear turned around

He headed back from where he'd come but please don't think him mean

Because that bear was never messy that bear's name was Clean

Now Clean he had an important job to clean up every mess

And Clean the bear he took that job very ser-i-ous

So every now and then someone like Messy found her way

Inside his belly - *"What how many?"* Only Clean can say

"And what about poor Messy Dad ... please tell me she's okay?"

No one knows she disappeared that same very day

It's bedtime now turn out the light tomorrows a new day

Where are you going?

"I'll be right back . . . just putting my clothes away."

FORGIVE and FORGET

Forgive he was a thoughtful boy who always tried to see

The happiness surrounding him and not the misery

He always did his best to understand his fellow man

And when let down he'd tell himself they did the best they can

Forgive he never held a grudge or stayed mad very long

Forgive he gave forgiveness unto each and every wrong

And when he did he'd say out loud with kindness in his eyes

"I forgive your meanness" or "your hurtfulness" or "lies"

"Forgiveness is a gift" he'd say "I give it to myself

Instead of holding anger in up high upon a shelf

I let it out the window where the wind blows it away

I find that when I do this I am happier each day

For life it is too short for us to stay mad very long

And each of us is filled inside with some right and some wrong

It's not my place to judge you for one single thing you did

I choose instead forgiveness now and hope that you will give

The same consideration when you find next time it's true

That you are on the receiving end of something hurting you"

And with everyone he said this to it was amazing just to see

How they learned forgiveness from the gift he gave for free

But sadly there was one who just refused and would not learn

Who never gave forgiveness and who let his anger burn

All the way deep down inside it never went away

It festered and it smoldered there growing day by day

"I won't forgive not now not ever!" he'd yell without regret

"I won't forgive I'll tell you why my name is Won't Forget"

"I won't forgive and I won't forget the bad things you've all done

I'll stay mad at each of you … each and every one!

Forgive he's simply wrong I don't know why none of you see

He lets those who have hurt him do exactly as they please

I'd rather remain angry so you all just stay away

Than take the risk of getting hurt by you again someday"

"It's sad that you would think that" Forgive said to Won't Forget

"It's sad that you would live like that, I think that I'd regret

All the chances that I'd missed to find out it was true

That the person hurting me had never even meant to

I hope you reconsider what it is you won't forget

I hope that you will just this once open up and let

All of us apologize and have the chance to say

How very truly sorry we are for hurting you this way

But Won't Forget he wouldn't listen and shooed them all away

He went to live all by himself he lives there still today

Angry and alone with no forgiveness in his life

Mad most of all though at himself and for all the strife

That he has caused unto himself by refusing to forgive

Cause Won't Forget he won't forget or himself forgive.

BEAUTY and UGLY

Quiet now children and settle in

For I have a tale to tell

It's a Beautifully Ugly fairy tale

So listen and listen well

Simmer down and gather round

As this learned tale begins

It's a story I tell of vanity

And why vanity never wins

Beauty was a princess in a kingdom long ago

And in this kingdom she grew up and up she sure did grow

She ended up 2 times the size a normal princess should

But who's to say what size is right or what size is good?

Her hair grew in a tangled mess with knots in every bit

Her tummy was a little round her back had a curve to it

Her arms were just a little short her hands had chubby fingers

Her eyes were just a little crooked her stare sometimes it lingered

Still Beauty was a beauty who had been named perfectly

Because her heart was beautiful for everyone to see

She always helped her friends whenever they had chores to do

She always helped her neighbors when they needed her help too

Beauty she was kind to every animal big and small

And Beauty always picked you up if ever you did fall

Beauty she gave compliments to friends and fam-il-y

And helped them all to see inside just how great they could be

She even took good care of the plants, bushes, flowers and trees

She watered and she weeded them and raked up all their leaves

Beauty she recycled things to save her Mother Earth

And Beauty almost always always thought of others first

But in the tiny kingdom where our princess Beauty lived

There also lived her brother who always used to give

His little sister Beauty a hard time it's sad but true

Prince Ugly acted ugly in almost everything he'd do

Still Ugly was a handsome Prince with muscles more than most

His hair was shiny golden as he always liked to boast

His skin was oh so smooth with not a pimple or a bump

His eyes they shone like diamonds even diamonds they would trump

His hands were smooth like glass with not a line there to be found

His head it was a perfect shape a perfect sort of round

His legs were strong and sturdy and much faster than the wind

Whenever he was in a race for sure that race he'd win

His feet they had 10 perfect toes with long and perfect nails

His lashes curved up perfectly just like in fairy tales

His arms they were both tan and lean in just the right proportion

Prince Ugly he was perfect looking without a sole distortion

But as I've said Prince Ugly he just wasn't very nice

He only thought about himself and his selfish life

He never went out of his way to help anyone else

He never even bothered much to think beyond himself

He never took a single day to water plants or trees

And never cared for Mother Earth or her creatures' needs

He never even helped a friend or a family member

Nor ever once a single neighbor not that I remember

Instead he choose to strut around and brag about his looks

And often said, "Hey look at me I think I wrote the book

On what it is to be so handsome, as handsome as can be

So if you fancy handsome well you must then fancy me"

Until one day the king of kings he came into the town

He'd left his giant castle where he'd ruled under his crown

For he was old and knew that now the time had come at last

To pass his kingdom to an heir before his time had passed

He took his crown and laid it down and rose up from his chair

"Beauty yes and Ugly too, both of you come here

I've watched you grow and studied you and how your lives have fared

I've given this a lot of thought and a lot of care

Beauty you shall be a queen and rule upon this land

For you have shown through kindness that you have a ruling hand

But Ugly don't despair my son I've not forgotten you

I have a gift for you as well a special gift it's true

For you a solid silver mirror a treasure from my youth

I want you now to gaze into it and see the ugly truth

This mirror it has helped me rule for all these many years

And kept my precious kingdom safe from oh so many tears

The mirror holds a wisdom that with reflection one can see

The mirror won't reflect at all that which is ugly

And many times its wisdom has from it to me been passed

When I'd look upon it and see nothing looking back

My hope for you my son is that with it you'll finally see

When it is that you have acted out of vanity"

So Ugly took hold of the mirror and looked into the glass

Expecting now to the see himself but suddenly he gasped

The mirror it held nothing . . . there was nothing there to see

For all he was was ugly . . . underneath ugly was he

But then there came an image that reflected in his place

An image of his sister and her softly smiling face

She'd come to stand beside him to support him with her grace

And wrapped her arms around him now in a lovingly embrace

And when he saw his sister there standing next to him

He realized her beauty lie well beneath her skin

"I'll do my best from now on father to try and make you proud

I've realized that acts of kindness they are what speak loud

About the kind of person . . . that other people see

About the kind of person . . . that I one day hope to be

And I agree you've chosen well a just queen has been found

I see it in her clearly now her beauty it abounds"

The king was simply overwhelmed and overjoyed to find

His son had learned his lesson well within such short a time

"I'm glad my son you've learned the truth and now you finally see

Your beauty comes from inside you and not from vanity"

And so our Beautifully Ugly tale it now comes to an end

Reminding us when judging things to always comprehend

That what we see on the surface . . . may not be all the proof

It's when we look within ourselves . . . that the mirror holds the truth.

SISTER and BROTHER

Sister said unto her Brother

"Brother I love you so

All my life no matter what

Together we will grow

Up and closer year by year

As we both come of age

Together read the book of life

Together turn each page

I love you so much Brother

I just wanted you to know

And so I wrote this poem for you

Hoping it will show

You just how much you mean to me

And how lucky I am

To have you as my brother

Throughout life to have your hand"

Brother looked down at his sister

Smiling up at him

And from each corner of his mouth

There slowly came a grin

Sister waited eagerly

As he began to speak

"Is that my pen and paper you've got?

You're not supposed to sneak

Into my room without permission

MOM SHE DID IT AGAIN!

For the last time Sister

Stay outta my room

… and give me back my pen!"

Sister dropped the pen and paper

As tears welled in her eyes

Her lips began to tremble

And a sob began to rise

"And one more thing"

Her Brother said

"I won't tell you again

I love you too

Now out with you

And go play with your friend."

This book is dedicated to my two nephews and my niece: Aidan, Isabella . . . and Maximilian, who never cease to awe and inspire me. A special thanks to friends and family for their comments, ideas and support.

Additional copies of this book are available at:

Recommended Direct Order Site:
https://www.createspace.com/4175136

or

www.amazon.com **by searching for the title:**

"Almost and Always"

www.ingramcontent.com/pod-product-compliance
Lightning Source LLC
LaVergne TN
LVHW010018070426
835512LV00001B/12